Power Maths

Year 1
Textbook 1B

White Rose Maths Edition

Ash

Ash is curious.

He likes to find out about new things.

helpful

Sparks

brave

Astrid

flexible

Flo

determined

Dexter

Series editor: Tony Staneff Lead author: Josh Lury
Consultant (first edition): Professor Liu Jian

Author team (first edition): Tony Staneff, Josh Lury, Beth Smith, Kelsey Brown, Jenny Lewis, Stephen Monaghan, Liu Jian, Zhou Da, Zhang Dan and Zhang Hong

Pearson

Contents

This shows us what page to turn to.

Are you ready to continue our maths journey?

How to use this book

Do you remember how to use Power Maths?

These pages help us get ready for a new unit.

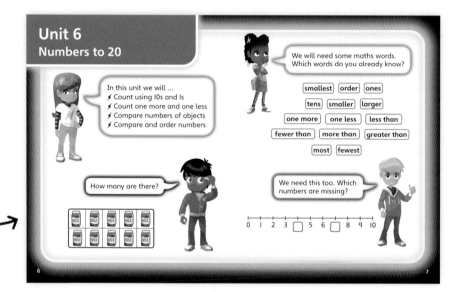

Discover

Lessons start with Discover.

Have fun exploring new maths problems.

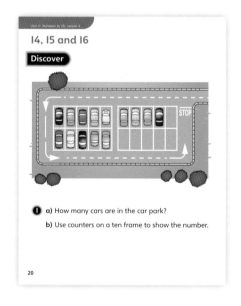

Share

Next, we share what we found out.

Did we all solve the problems the same way?

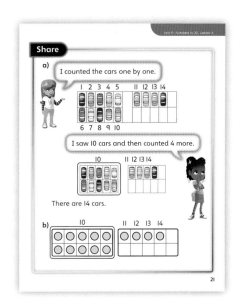

Think together

Then we have a go at some more problems together.

We will try a challenge too!

This tells you which page to go to in your Practice Book.

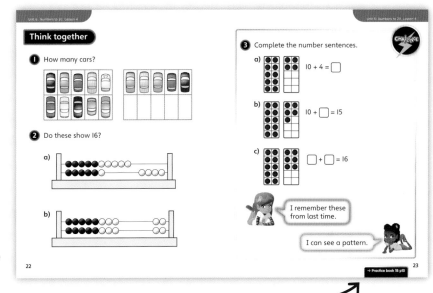

At the end of a unit we will show how much we can do!

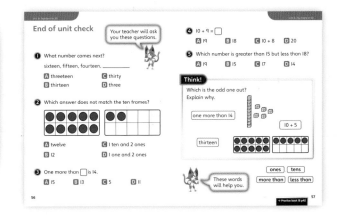

Unit 6
Numbers to 20

In this unit we will ...
- ⚡ Count using 10s and 1s
- ⚡ Count one more and one less
- ⚡ Compare numbers of objects
- ⚡ Compare and order numbers

How many are there?

We will need some maths words. Which words do you already know?

smallest order ones

tens smaller larger

one more one less less than

fewer than more than greater than

most fewest

We need this too. Which numbers are missing?

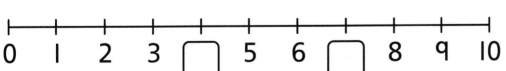

0 1 2 3 ☐ 5 6 ☐ 8 9 10

Count to 20

Discover

1 **a)** Count as a class from 1 to 20.

b) Count how many children are in the class.

Share

a)

b)

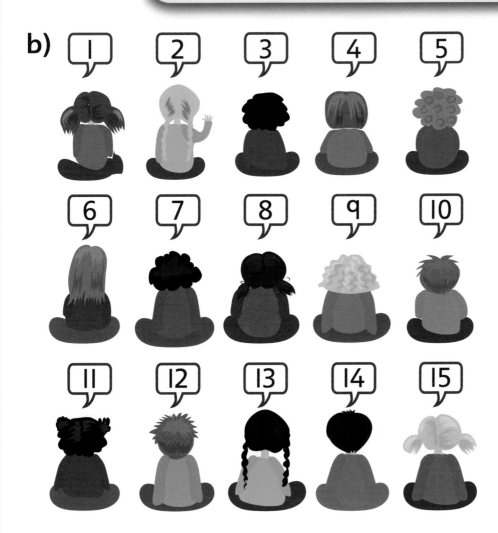

There are 15 children in the class.

Think together

1 Continue the count.

2 How many ladybirds?

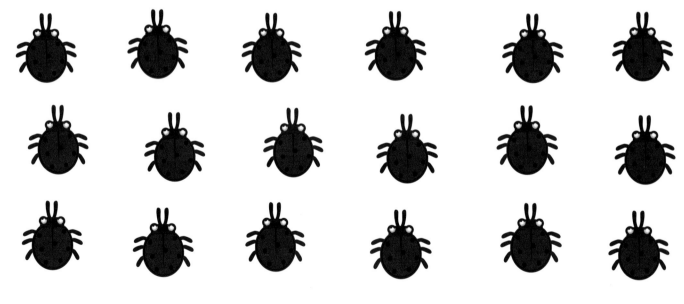

I wonder how I can make sure I don't miss any.

3 Complete the number tracks.

a)

| 8 | 9 | | 11 | 12 | | | 15 |

b)

| 12 | 13 | | | | | | |

c)

| 20 | 19 | 18 | | | | | |

These are easy if I know the count.

I think one of them goes backwards.

11

Understand 10

Discover

1 **a)** Will and Katy have put counters onto the ten frame.

How do you know there are 10 without counting?

b) Show 10 in different ways.

Share

a)

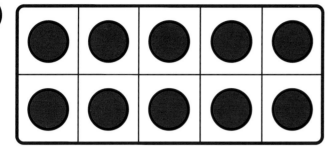

The ten frame is full so I knew there were 10. I didn't need to count.

b)

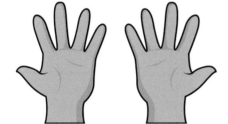

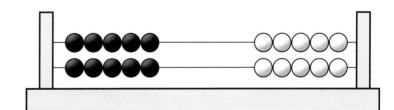

Think together

1 Use cubes or counters.

Fill the ten frame to show 10.

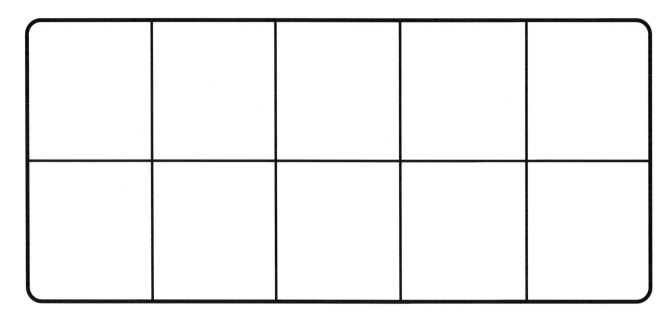

2 Tell a partner where you can see 10.

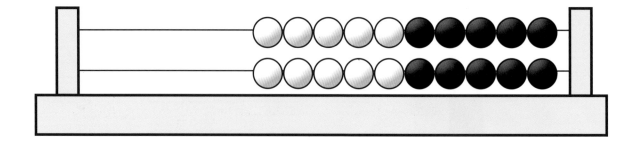

3 In each pair, which image shows 10?

a)

 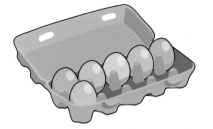

b)

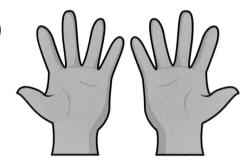 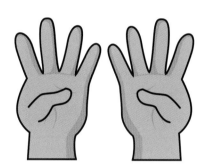

c)

I can spot 10 without counting.

I wonder what the other pictures show.

15

11, 12 and 13

Discover

Seth

Rosa

1 **a)** How many eggs will fill the box?

b) How many eggs are on the tray?

Share

a) 10 eggs will fill the box.

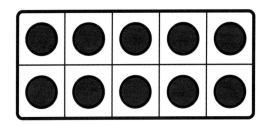

I noticed the egg box looks like the ten frame.

b) Use counters to represent the eggs and put them on a ten frame.

There are 10 in the box and I more.

I **more than** 10 is 11.

There are 11 eggs on the tray.

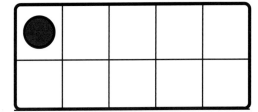

I remember, when counting, the next number after 10 is 11.

Think together

1 How many eggs?

I don't think I have to count all the eggs in the box.

2 What number is shown?

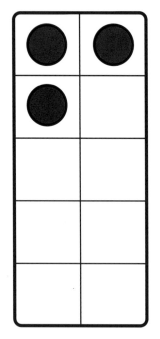

3 What can you see?

CHALLENGE

$$10 + 1 = 11$$

$$10 + 2 = 12$$

$$10 + 3 = 13$$

Explain the number sentences to a partner.

I can see from the first picture why 10 + 1 is equal to 11.

These numbers are all 10 and a bit more.

19

→ Practice book 1B p12

14, 15 and 16

Discover

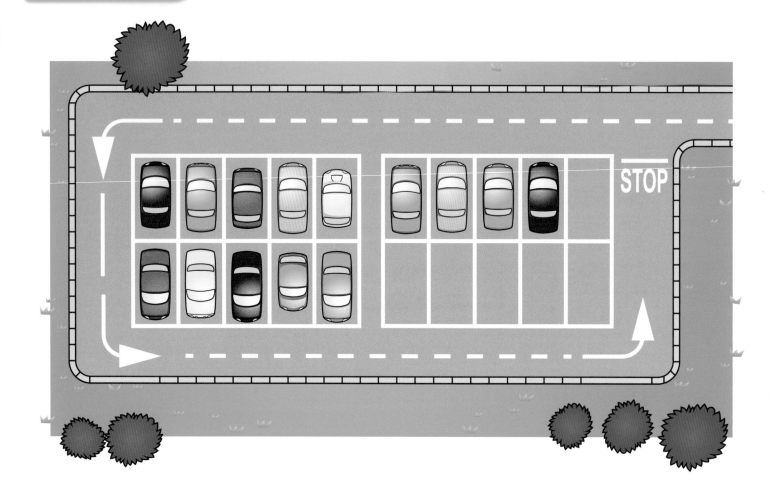

1 **a)** How many cars are in the car park?

b) Use counters on a ten frame to show the number.

Share

a)

I counted the cars one by one.

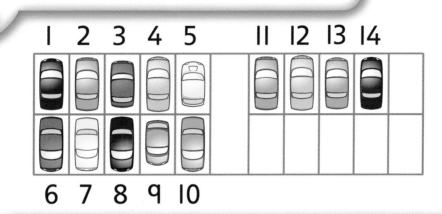

I saw 10 cars and then counted 4 more.

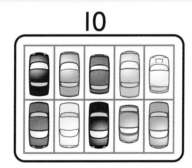

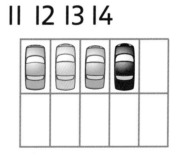

There are 14 cars.

b)

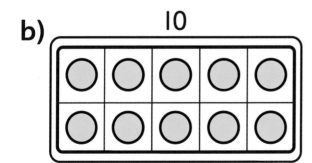

Think together

1 How many cars?

 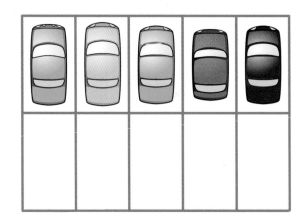

2 Do these show 16?

a)

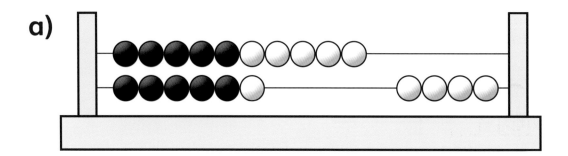

b)

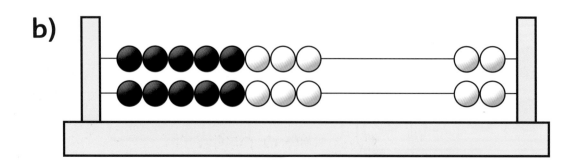

3 Complete the number sentences.

a) 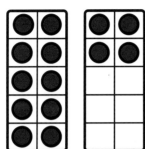 $10 + 4 = \boxed{}$

b) 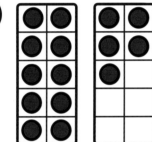 $10 + \boxed{} = 15$

c) 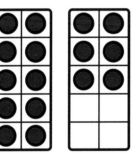 $\boxed{} + \boxed{} = 16$

I remember these from last time.

I can see a pattern.

23

17, 18 and 19

Discover

1 **a)** What number have the children made?

b) Show 18 and 19 on ten frames.

Share

a)

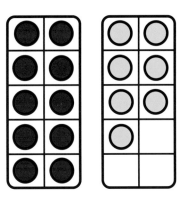

I could see a full 10 and 7 more. I didn't need to count.

10 + 7 = 17

The number is 17.

I wonder if there are other ways to represent the numbers.

b)

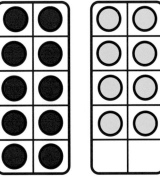

10 + 8 = 18

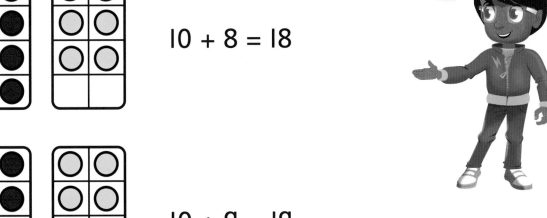

10 + 9 = 19

Think together

1 What numbers do these show?

a)

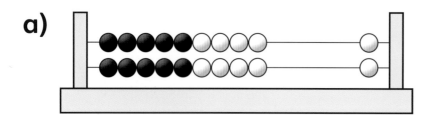

b)

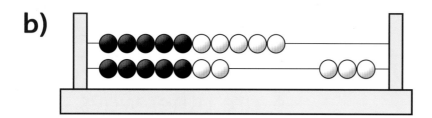

2 Here is 19.

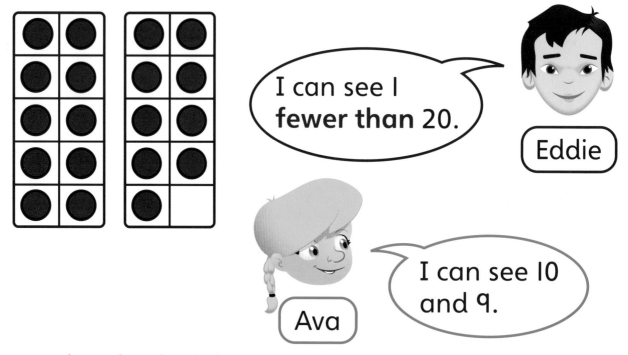

I can see 1 fewer than 20.

Eddie

I can see 10 and 9.

Ava

Are they both right?

CHALLENGE

 3 Complete the number sentences.

10 + 1 = ☐

10 + 2 = ☐

10 + 3 = ☐

10 + 4 = ☐

10 + 5 = ☐

10 + 6 = ☐

10 + 7 = ☐

10 + 8 = ☐

10 + 9 = ☐

I think these are all the numbers from 11 to 19.

All the number sentences start with 10.

What is the same? What is different?

27

→ Practice book 1B p18

Understand 20

Discover

Bo   Kat

1 **a)** Are the children showing 20?

b) Show 20 using counters on two ten frames.

Share

a)

The children are showing **2 tens**. I know that 2 tens make 20.

Bo is showing 10.

Kat is showing 10.

They are showing 20 in total.

b) Fill two ten frames.

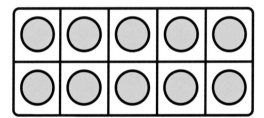

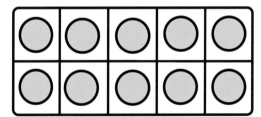

This shows 20.

I know that two full ten frames make 20. I don't need to count.

29

Think together

1 Do these ten frames show 20?

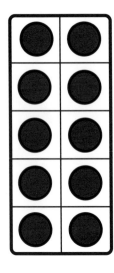 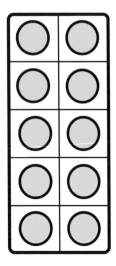

2 Which rekenrek shows 20?

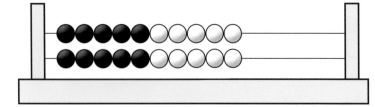

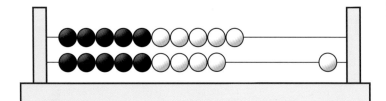

I wonder what number the other rekenrek shows.

3 Make or show 20 in different ways.

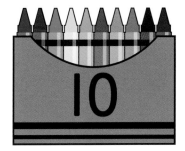 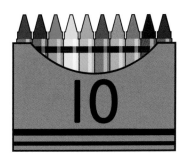

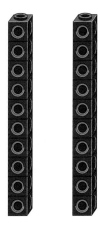

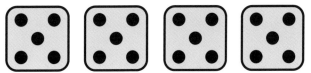

I can make 20 in some of these ways.

I can think of some more ways.

31

One more and one less

Discover

1 **a)** How many children are in the line?

Show this using counters and ten frames.

b) One more child joins.

How many now?

Share

a)

1   2   3   4   5   6   7   8   9   10   11   12

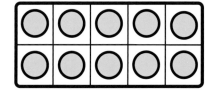

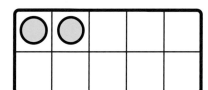

I know that 12 is 10 + 2.

b) One more child joins.

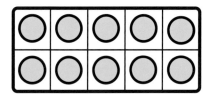

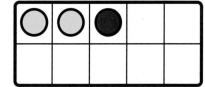

I added one more counter to my ten frames.

There is now 10 + 3, which is 13.

So one more than 12 is 13.

Think together

1. Complete these sentences.

a) One more than 14 is ☐.

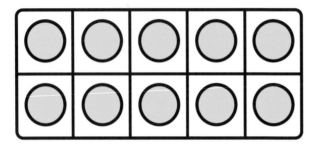 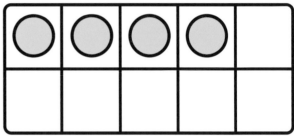

b) One more than 17 is ☐.

2. Complete these sentences.

a) One **less than** 17 is ☐.

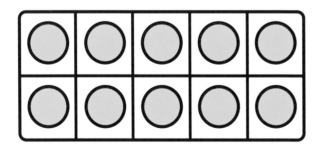 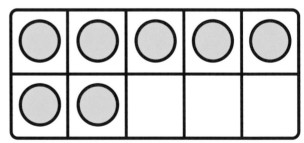

b) One less than 11 is ☐.

34

3 Complete.

a)

I more

15 → ☐

b)

I more

19 → ☐

c)

I less

☐ ← 13

If I know my numbers to 20 these are easier to work out.

35

→ Practice book 1B p24

The number line to 20

Discover

1 **a)** What numbers will the next two shirts on the washing line be?

b) Write the shirt numbers in **order**, from 11 to 20.

Share

a)

I know that 14 and 15 come next when I count on from 11.

b)

This looks like a number line from 11 to 20.

Think together

1 Count up in order. Point to the numbers as you count.

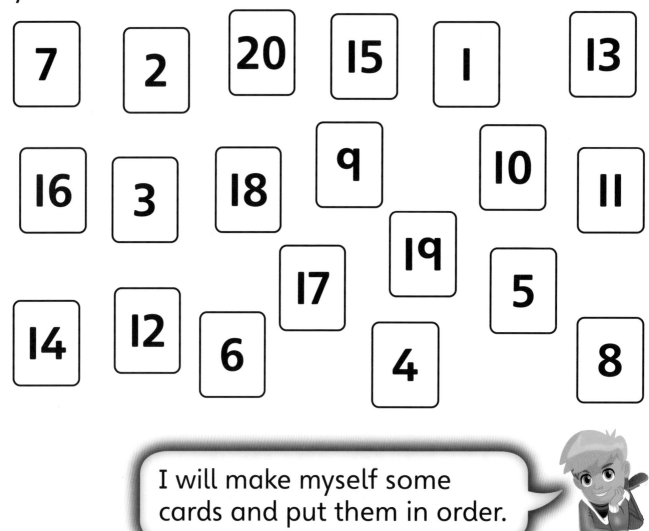

I will make myself some cards and put them in order.

2 Here is a number line.

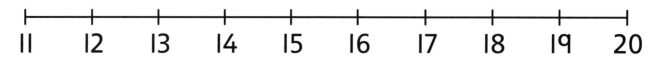

Say and point to the numbers.

3 Continue the number lines.

CHALLENGE

0 1 2 3 4 5 6

20
19
18
17
16
15

These number lines look different.

But I think they show the same numbers.

39

→ Practice book 1B p27

Label number lines

Discover

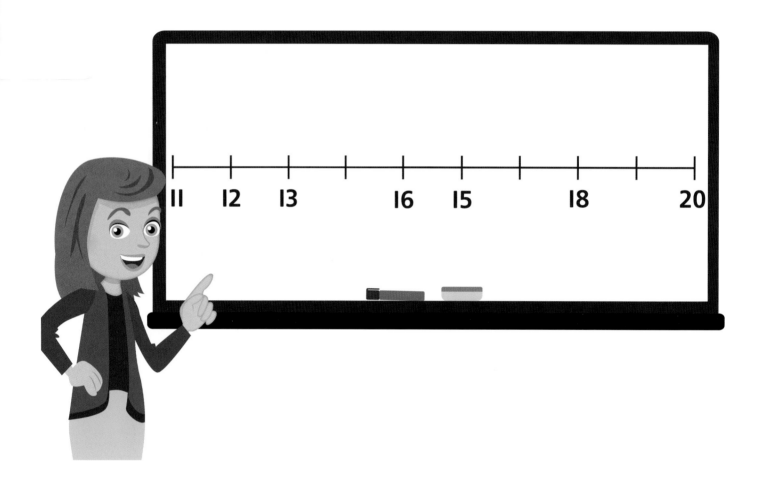

1 a) Which two numbers are the wrong way around?

b) What are the missing numbers?

Share

a)

15 and 16 are the wrong way around.

b)

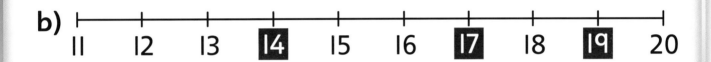

I knew how to count from 11 to 20. This helped me work out the missing numbers.

Think together

1 What are the missing numbers?

a)

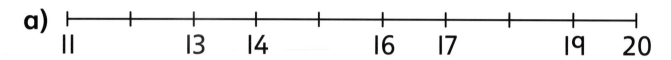

11   13   14   16   17   19   20

b)

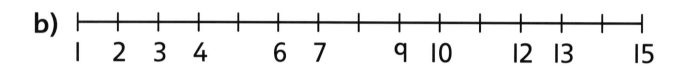

1   2   3   4   6   7   9   10   12   13   15

2 Where should each number go on the number line?

13   15   19

11   20

3 Point to where the number 17 goes on each number line.

I think it will go in a different place on each line.

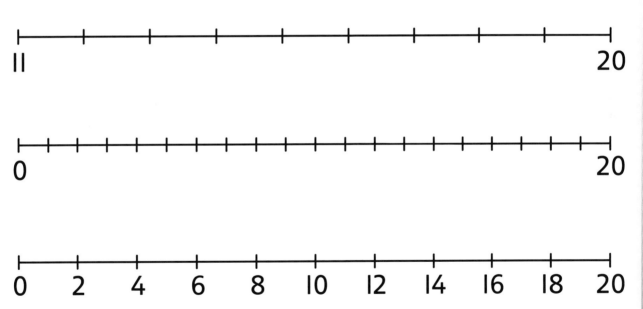

11   20

0   20

0   2   4   6   8   10   12   14   16   18   20

I think it goes between two numbers on the last number line.

43

Estimate on a number line

Discover

1 **a)** Where should Danny stand?

b) Where should Meg stand?

Share

a) Danny's number is 15.

15 more than 10 but less than 20.

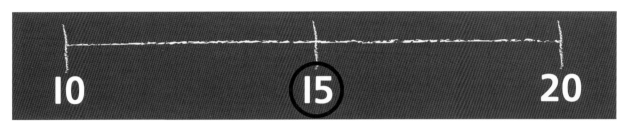

15 is in the middle of 10 and 20.

b) Meg's number is 19.

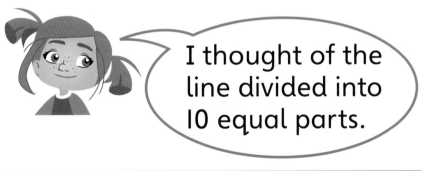

I thought of the line divided into 10 equal parts.

Count on in 1s from 10 or back in 1s from 20.

Think together

1 **a)** Point to the number 16 on this line.

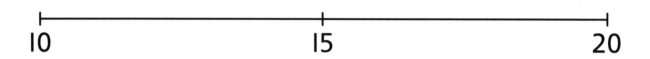

b) Point to the number 11 on the line.

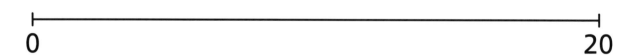

2 Estimate the numbers the arrows are pointing to.

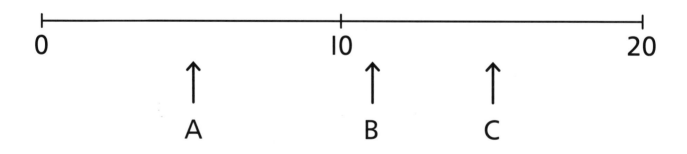

3 Estimate where the number 19 goes on each line.

CHALLENGE

a)

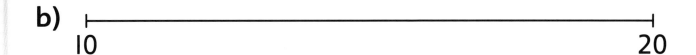

0   20

b)

10   20

Which line was easier to estimate?

Which was the most difficult?

I can see that the two number lines start at different numbers.

19 is close to 20. Maybe I will put 19 in the same place on both lines.

47

Compare numbers to 20

Discover

Jack

Kendi

1 a) How many marbles does Jack have?

How many does Kendi have?

b) Who has more marbles?

Share

a) Jack has 14 marbles.

Kendi has 11 marbles.

Jack has 10 in the bag and 4 more. I know that 10 + 4 is 14.

b)

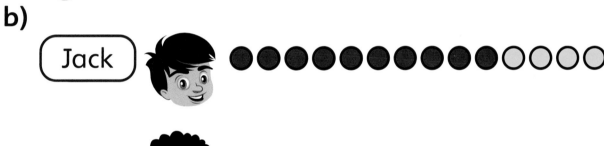

Jack has more marbles than Kendi.

I lined up the marbles. I can easily see Jack has more than Kendi.

We can say that 14 > 11.

Think together

1 Who has fewer?

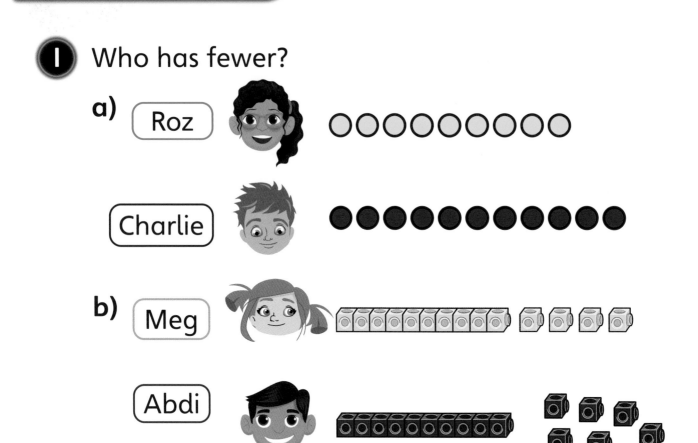

a) Roz

Charlie

b) Meg

Abdi

2 Which film has more votes?

	Votes
Dino Adventure	① ② ③ ④ ⑤ ⑥ ⑦ ⑧ ⑨ ⑩ ⑪ ⑫ ⑬ ⑭ ⑮
Space Fun	① ② ③ ④ ⑤ ⑥ ⑦ ⑧ ⑨ ⑩ ⑪ ⑫ ⑬ ⑭ ⑮ ⑯ ⑰ ⑱

3 **a)** Which is the **smaller** number?

| 15 | 19 |

Prove it!

b) Which is the **larger** number?

| 20 | 9 |

Prove it!

I will make each number using cubes to compare.

I will use a number line to help me.

I will compare the numbers using < or > symbols.

51

→ Practice book 1B p36

Order numbers to 20

Discover

Anya   Bo   Cal

1 **a)** Order the number of sweets from fewest to most.

b) Who has the most sweets?

Share

a)

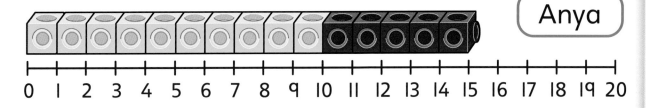

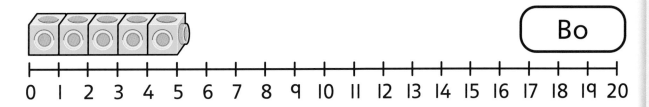

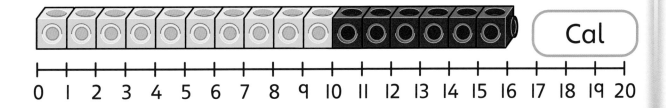

5 is less than 15.

15 is less than 16.

5 < 15 < 16

I used a number line to put them in order.

b) 16 is **greater than** 5.

16 is greater than 15.

Cal has the most sweets.

Think together

1 Put the numbers 16, 19 and 12 in order.

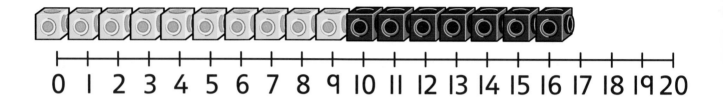

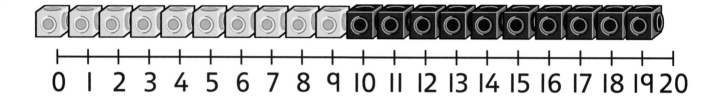

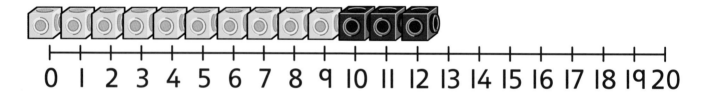

☐ is less than ☐

☐ is less than ☐

☐ < ☐ < ☐

2 Order the numbers, starting with the **smallest**.

14   16   13

☐ < ☐ < ☐

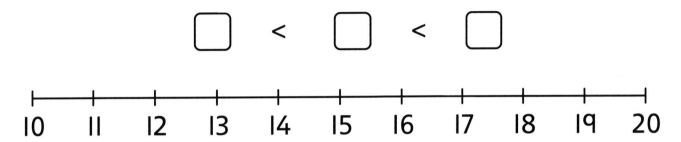

3 Which numbers could go in the boxes?

CHALLENGE

13 < ☐ < 17   17 > ☐ > 13

13 < 17 < ☐

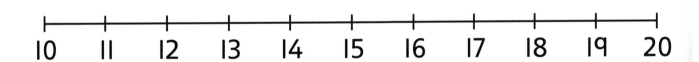

I wonder if there is more than one answer.

55

End of unit check

Your teacher will ask you these questions.

1 What number comes next?

sixteen, fifteen, fourteen, _____

A threeteen

B thirteen

C thirty

D three

2 Which answer does not match the ten frames?

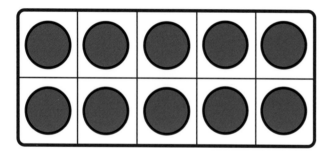
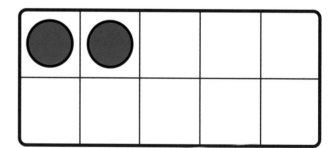

A twelve

B 12

C 1 ten and 2 ones

D 1 one and 2 ones

3 One more than ▢ is 14.

A 15

B 13

C 5

D 11

4 10 + 9 = ☐

A 19　　　　B 18　　　　C 10 + 8　　　D 20

5 Which number is greater than 15 but less than 18?

A 19　　　　B 15　　　　C 17　　　　D 14

Think!

Which is the odd one out?
Explain why.

one more than 14

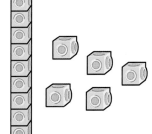

10 + 5

thirteen

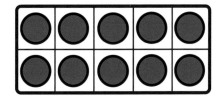

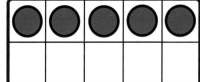

These words will help you.

ones　　tens

more than　　less than

57

→ Practice book 1B p42

Unit 7
Addition and subtraction within 20

In this unit we will ...

⚡ Add and subtract by counting on or back

⚡ Add and subtract using number bonds

⚡ Use doubles and near doubles

⚡ Find a difference

⚡ Solve word problems

How can you use a ten frame to add 8 red counters and 5 yellow counters?

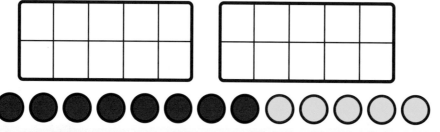

We will need some maths words. Which words do you already know?

add   altogether   subtract

difference   how many are left?

fact family   how many fewer?

number bonds

We can use a number line and a number track to help us add and subtract. What is 13 – 3?

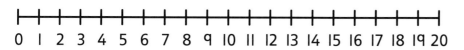

0 1 2 3 4 5 6 7 8 9 10 11 12 13 14 15 16 17 18 19 20

1 2 3 4 5 6 7 8 9 10 11 12 13 14 15 16 17 18 19 20

Add by counting on within 20

Discover

1 **a)** How many children are on the bus?

b) There are 3 more children waiting.

How many children are there in total?

Share

a)

There are 8 children on the bus.

You don't need to count the children on the bus again.

b)

First there are 8 children on the bus.

3 more children are waiting.

8 + 3 = 11

There are 11 children in total.

Think together

1 Add by counting on.

a)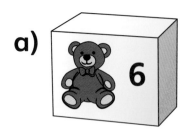

6 + 2 = ☐

b)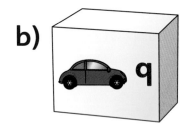

9 + 2 = ☐

c)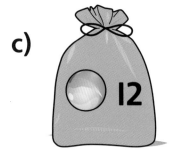

12 + 2 = ☐

2 Use the number line to complete the additions.

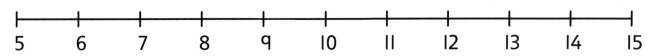

5   6   7   8   9   10   11   12   13   14   15

a) $6 + 3 = \square$

b) $7 + 7 = \square$

c) $9 + 4 = \square$

d) $12 + 3 = \square$

3 Hassan is working out $3 + 9$.

CHALLENGE

I started at 9 and counted on 3.

Hassan

9

10   11   12

Use Hassan's method to solve these additions.

$2 + 9 = \square$ $3 + 14 = \square$ $2 + 16 = \square$

63

→ Practice book 1B p44

Add ones using number bonds

Discover

1. **a)** A full box holds 10 ✂.

   How many ✂ are in the boxes?

   b) Rani adds 3 more ✂.

   How many are there now?

Share

a)

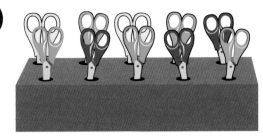

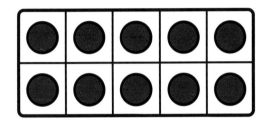
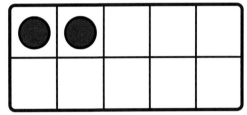

There are 12 ✂ in the boxes.

b)

12 is 10 and 2.

12 + 3 = 15

There are 15 ✂ now.

2 + 3 = 5,
so 12 + 3 = 15.

65

Think together

1 Solve 15 + 4

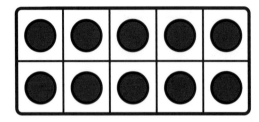 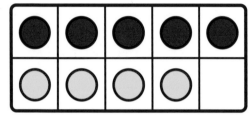

5 + 4 = ☐

So

15 + 4 = ☐

I will work out 5 + 4 first.

2 **a)** Solve 13 + 2

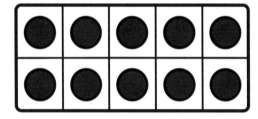 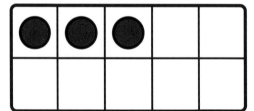

3 + 2 = ☐

So

13 + 2 = ☐

b) Now try 14 + 3 = ☐

I will make 14 on two ten frames.

 a) Find solutions to this problem.

$$\boxed{1}\,\boxed{} \;+\; \boxed{} \;=\; \boxed{18}$$

b) Find solutions to this problem.

$$\boxed{1}\,\boxed{} \;+\; \boxed{} \;=\; \boxed{15}$$

I will try to find more than three ways.

First, I will work out bonds for 8. 1 + 7 = 8. 2 + 6 = 8 ... 8 + 0 = 8.

67

Find and make number bonds to 20

Discover

1 **a)** How many red cubes?

How many yellow cubes?

How many altogether?

b) Show another **number bond** to 20.

Share

a)

There are 10 red cubes.   There are 10 yellow cubes.

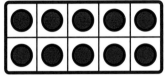 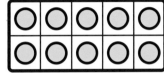

10 + 10 = 20

There are 20 cubes altogether.

b) Two ten frames can show number bonds to 20.

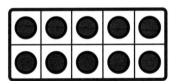 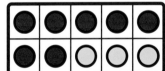

7 + 3 = 10

So

17 + 3 = 20

I know bonds to 10, so I also know bonds to 20.

Did you find different number bonds?

69

Think together

1 Complete the number bond to 20.

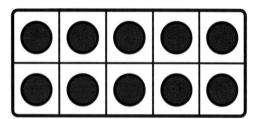 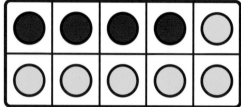

$4 + 6 = 10$

So

 $\boxed{} + \boxed{} = 20$

I will work out the bond to 10 first.

2 Complete the number bond to 10.

$\boxed{} + \boxed{} = 10$

Use this number bond to find two different bonds to 20.

3 **a)** Complete the number bonds to 20.

CHALLENGE

$1 + \boxed{} = 20$

$2 + \boxed{} = 20$

$3 + \boxed{} = 20$

$11 + \boxed{} = 20$

$12 + \boxed{} = 20$

$13 + \boxed{} = 20$

$\boxed{} + 9 = 20$

$\boxed{} + 19 = 20$

How do the bonds to 20 link to the bonds to 10?

I think these could be written in pairs.

b) Can you list all the bonds to 20?

71

Doubles

Discover

Play the mirror game.

I showed I.

So I show I too.

Ali

Zac

1 **a)** How many fingers in total?

b) Play this mirror game with a partner.

Use one hand each.

Find all the doubles.

Share

a) They are both showing 1. This is double 1.

Double 1   $1 + 1 = 2$

There are 2 fingers in total.

b)

Double 2   $2 + 2 = 4$

Double 3   $3 + 3 = 6$

Double 4   $4 + 4 = 8$

Double 5   $5 + 5 = 10$

Think together

1 **a)** Which are doubles? Which are not doubles?

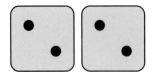 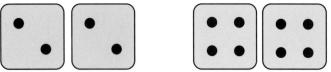 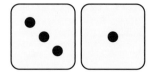

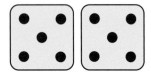 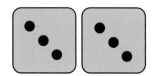 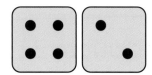

b) Work out the score of each double.

2 Work out the score of double 6.

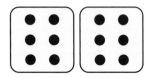

6 + 6 = ☐

Now let's play a game.

See if we can roll doubles and call out the score.

3 Work out

CHALLENGE

double 6

6 + 6 = ☐

double 7

7 + 7 = ☐

I wonder if there's a way to work out all of these doubles.

double 8

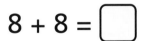

8 + 8 = ☐

double 9

9 + 9 = ☐

I know double 10 already!

→ Practice book 1B p53

Near doubles

Discover

1 a) Use some cubes. Make towers to show 5 + 5.

Now change them to show 5 + 6.

b) Work out 3 + 3. Now work out 3 + 4.

Share

a) $5 + 5$ $5 + 6$

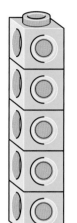 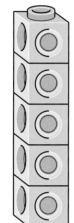   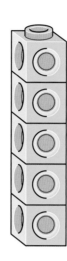 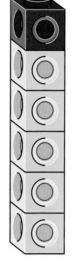

So if I know 5 + 5 is 10, I know 5 + 6 is 11.

5 + 5 is a double. 5 + 6 is one more.

b) $3 + 3$ $3 + 4$

 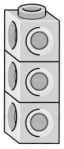   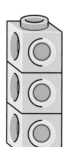 

$3 + 3 = 6$ so $3 + 4 = 7$

Think together

1 Change fingers to turn doubles into near doubles.

2 + 2 = 4   So   2 + 3 = ☐

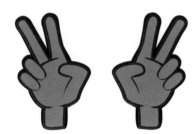

4 + 4 = 8   So   4 + 5 = ☐

2 Complete the doubles and near doubles.

1 + 1 = ☐   6 + 6 = ☐   9 + 9 = ☐

1 + 2 = ☐   6 + 7 = ☐   9 + 10 = ☐

2 + 1 = ☐   7 + 6 = ☐   10 + 9 = ☐

3 **a)** Point to double 5 on the number line.

Point to double 6.

Point to 5 + 6.

What do you notice?

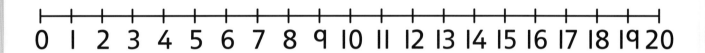

0 1 2 3 4 5 6 7 8 9 10 11 12 13 14 15 16 17 18 19 20

b) Work out these near doubles.

2 + 3 = ☐   6 + 5 = ☐

5 + 4 = ☐   9 + 8 = ☐

7 + 8 = ☐   8 + 9 = ☐

I will point to the closest double to help me.

79

→ Practice book 1B p56

Subtract ones using number bonds

Discover

I **a)** How many footballs are there in total?

b) They kick 3 away.

How many are left?

Share

a)

There are 15 footballs in total.

b) First there were 15, then 3 were kicked away.

I crossed out 3 footballs and counted how many were left.

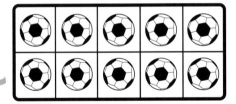

I know that 5 − 3 = 2, so 15 − 3 = 12.

15 − 3 = 12

There are 12 footballs left.

Think together

1 **a)** Work out 19 – 6.

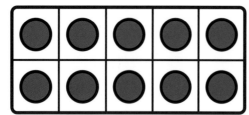 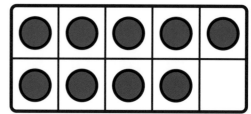

19 – 6 = ☐

b) Work out 16 – 4.

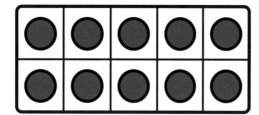 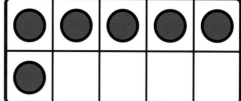

16 – 4 = ☐

2 There are 16 leaves on the tree.

5 leaves fall to the ground.

How many leaves are there left on the tree?

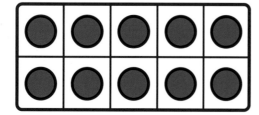

16 – 5 = ☐

3 Work out the missing numbers in these number sentences.

a) 7 – 5 = ☐

17 – 5 = ☐

I think I can use 7 – 5 to help me work out 17 – 5.

b) 8 – 3 = ☐

☐ – 3 = 15

c) 7 – ☐ = 0

☐ – 7 = 10

I will think about what would make the answer to a **subtraction** 0.

83

Subtraction – count back

Discover

1 **a)** How many pencils does Mrs Hill have?

b) The teacher gives each child a pencil.

How many pencils does she have left?

Share

a) Mrs Hill has a box of 10 pencils and 3 pencils.

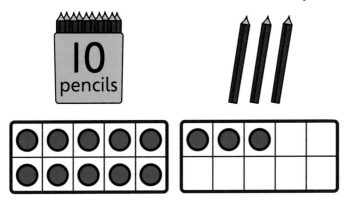

Mrs Hill has 13 pencils.

b) There are 5 children.

Mrs Hill gives each child a pencil.

Work out 13 − 5.

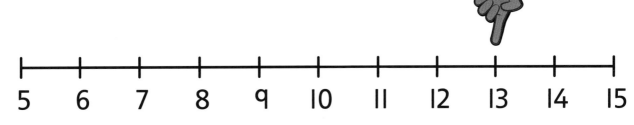

Start on 13. Count back 5 jumps.

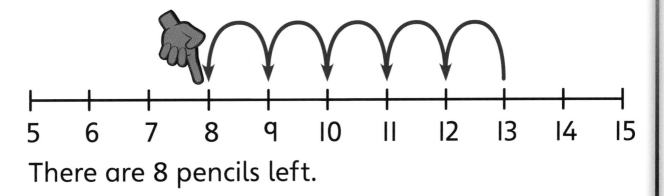

There are 8 pencils left.

Think together

1 Work out the subtraction.

11 − 2 = ☐

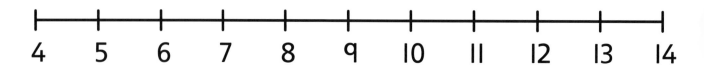

2 Work out the subtractions.

a) 12 − 3 = ☐

b) 14 − 1 = ☐

c) 15 − 7 = ☐

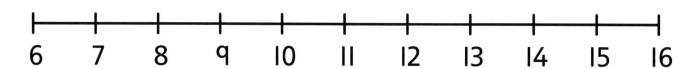

> I will use some counters and two ten frames. I will cross out the counters that I subtract.

3 **a)** Work out

18 − 10 = ☐

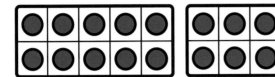

16 − 10 = ☐

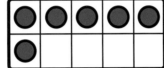

15 − 10 = ☐

Tell a partner what you notice.

b) Work out 18 − 15.

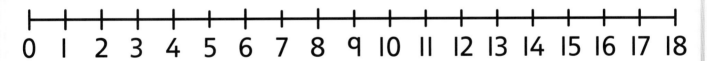

0 1 2 3 4 5 6 7 8 9 10 11 12 13 14 15 16 17 18

I'm going to subtract 10 then 5.

I wonder if I can jump back 10 quickly or use ten frames.

CHALLENGE

87

→ Practice book 1B p62

Subtraction – find the difference

Discover

1 **a)** **How many more** children are in the back row than the front row?

b) **How many fewer** children are in the front row than the back row?

Share

a)

You can count on or count back to find the **difference**.

$8 - 6 = 2$

There are 2 more children in the back row.

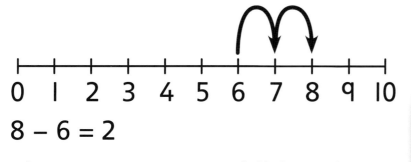

b)

Now I know how many more, I also know how many fewer.

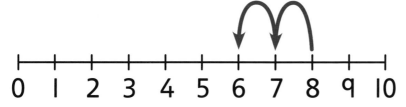

There are 2 fewer children in the front row.

The difference is 2.

Think together

1 How many more children are in the front row?

☐ − ☐ = ☐

2 How many fewer counters are there in the top row?

☐ − ☐ = ☐

3 Amy, Danny and Hassan are working out $15 - 14 = \boxed{}$.

CHALLENGE

I will count back 14 on a number line.

I will cross out counters on two ten frames.

I will find the difference between 15 and 14.

Amy

Danny

Hassan

a) Talk to a partner about the different methods.

b) Find the difference to solve these subtractions.

$13 - 11 = \boxed{}$

$17 - 16 = \boxed{}$

$20 - 17 = \boxed{}$

91

→ Practice book 1B p65

Related facts – fact families

Discover

1 **a)** How many fingers are the children holding up?

⬜ + ⬜ = ⬜

b) Work out the missing numbers.

13 + ⬜ = 20

⬜ + 13 = 20

Share

a)

$8 + 10 = 18$

$10 + 8 = 18$

Add in any order. The total stays the same.

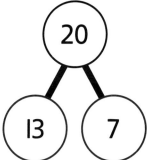

b) $13 + 7 = 20$

$7 + 13 = 20$

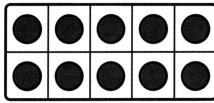 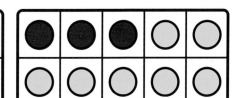

I can add $7 + 13$, or $13 + 7$.

Think together

1 Complete the fact family.

6 + 4 = ☐

4 + 6 = ☐

10 − 4 = ☐

10 − 6 = ☐

Fact families contain all the same numbers.

2

12 + ☐ = 15

☐ + ☐ = 15

☐ − ☐ = ☐

☐ − ☐ = ☐

3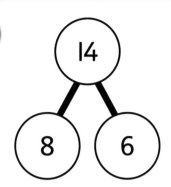

a) Show this part-whole model using two ten frames or a bead string.

b) Complete the fact family.

☐ + ☐ = ☐   ☐ − ☐ = ☐

☐ + ☐ = ☐   ☐ − ☐ = ☐

I can work out eight facts.

I thought there were only four.

95

Missing number problems

Discover

1 **a)** What is the missing number?

$4 + $ ✹ $= 6$

b) What is the missing number?

✹ $+ 1 = 6$

Share

a) $4 + $  $= 6$

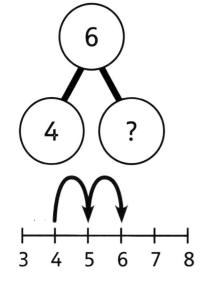

I thought about it as 4 add something is 6.

4 + 2 is 6.

The missing number is 2.

b)  $+ 1 = 6$

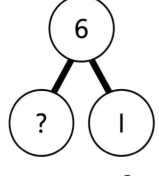

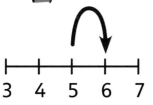

I thought about it as something add 1 is 6.

5 + 1 more is 6.

The missing number is 5.

Think together

1 Use the part-whole model to work out the missing numbers.

$11 + \boxed{} = 20$

$9 + \boxed{} = 20$

$20 - \boxed{} = 11$

$20 - \boxed{} = 9$

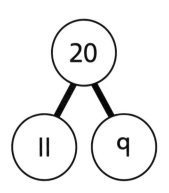

2 Use the number line to work out the missing numbers.

$6 + \boxed{} = 9$

$6 + \boxed{} = 11$

$12 - \boxed{} = 8$

$12 - 8 = \boxed{}$

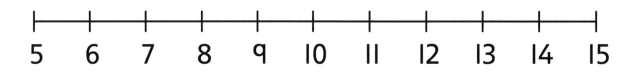

3 **a)** Work out the missing numbers.

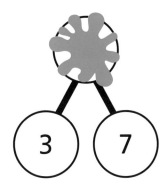

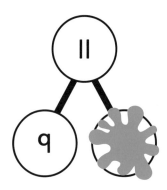

3 + 7 = ✹

7 + 3 = ✹

✹ – 3 = 7

✹ – 7 = 3

9 + ✹ = 11

✹ + 9 = 11

11 – ✹ = 9

11 – 9 = ✹

I can use counters or drawings to work out the missing whole or part.

b) Now try these.

5 + ✹ = 9

✹ – 5 = 8

✹ + 4 = 17

19 – ✹ = 10

99

Solve word and picture problems – addition and subtraction

Discover

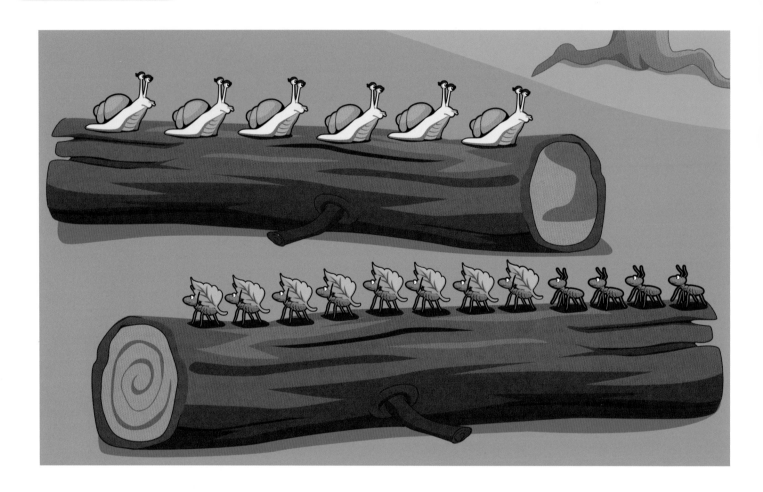

1 **a)** How many ants are there in total?

b) There are 19 snails inside the log.

How many more snails are there inside the log than on the log?

Share

a) There are 8 ants carrying a leaf.

There are 4 ants not carrying a leaf.

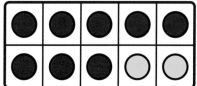 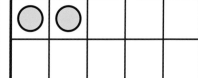

8 + 4 = 12

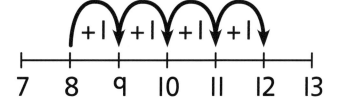

There are 12 ants in total.

b) There are 19 snails inside the log.

There are 6 snails on the log.

19 − 6 = 13

There are 13 more snails inside the log than on the log.

To work out how many more we must find the difference. This is a subtraction.

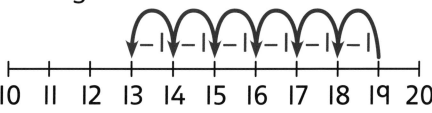

Think together

1 There are 14 bees in a hive. 6 bees fly away.

How many bees are there left in the hive?

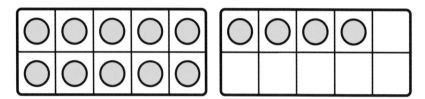

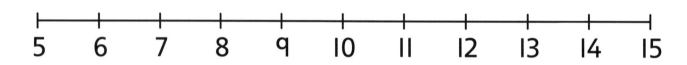

There are ☐ bees left in the hive.

2 How many spots are there altogether?

☐ + ☐ = ☐

There are ☐ spots altogether.

3

There are 17 stars in the box.

a) 12 stars are removed. How many stars are left in the box?

There are ☐ stars left in the box.

b) 12 stars are gold. The rest are silver.

How many silver stars are there?

There are ☐ silver stars.

c) There are also 12 coins in the box.

How many more stars than coins are there?

There are ☐ more stars than coins.

d) What is the same about the questions and answers?

→ Practice book 1B p74

End of unit check

1 Milo has 6 counters.

Izzy has 7 counters.

Your teacher will ask you these questions.

How many counters are there altogether?

A 6 + 7 = 12

C 6 + 7 = 13

B 6 + 7 = 14

D 6 + 7 = 17

2 16 − 4 = ☐

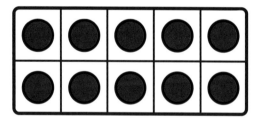 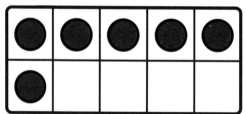

A 20   **B** 13   **C** 2   **D** 12

3 Find the difference between 12 and 4.

A 16   **B** 6   **C** 8   **D** 7

4 $11 + 9 = 20$

Which of these facts is **not** correct?

A $9 + 11 = 20$ **C** $20 = 11 + 9$

B $20 - 9 = 11$ **D** $11 - 20 = 9$

5 What is the missing number in both boxes?

$13 - \boxed{} = 6$ $15 = 8 + \boxed{}$

A 19   **B** 7   **C** 6   **D** 8

Think!

$10 = \stackrel{\LARGE\bigstar}{} + 7$ $20 - \stackrel{\LARGE\bigstar}{} = \triangle$ $\triangle + 1 = \boxed{}$

First I worked out what ☆ was by ...

Then, I worked out what △ was by ...

Then, I worked out what ☐ was by ...

What is ☐ ?

These words might help you.

adding   ten   subtracting

twenty   bond   more

→ Practice book 1B p77

Unit 8
Numbers to 50

In this unit we will ...
- ⚡ Count up to 50
- ⚡ Compare numbers to 50
- ⚡ Order numbers
- ⚡ Count in 2s and 5s
- ⚡ Solve word and picture problems

We can use a number line to help us order and compare numbers. Which number is larger, 12 or 21?

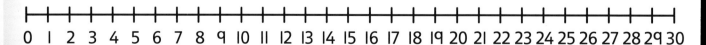

0 1 2 3 4 5 6 7 8 9 10 11 12 13 14 15 16 17 18 19 20 21 22 23 24 25 26 27 28 29 30

We will need some maths words and signs.
Do you remember these?

ones   tens   compare

order   less than (<)

greater than (>)

We can use different equipment to show the value of a number. We can use cubes, bead strings, ten frames or rekenreks. What number is shown here?

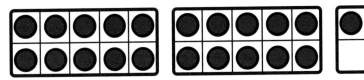
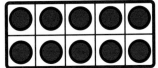
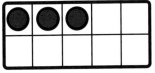

Count to 50

Discover

1 **a)** Count the jars.

b) Count from 30 to 50 with a partner, or as a class.

Share

a)

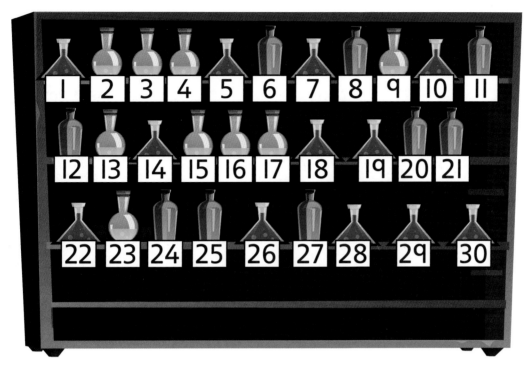

I started counting from the top row.

There are 30 jars.

b)

31	32	33	34	35	36	37	38	39	40

41	42	43	44	45	46	47	48	49	50

Think together

1 How many ladybirds?

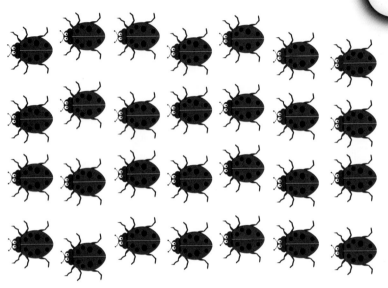

I wonder how I can make sure I don't miss any.

2 What are the missing numbers?

a)

 23 24 25

b)

40		42	43	

c)

28			31		33

There are 50 sweets in the jar.

Take one sweet out.

How many sweets are there now?

Take one more sweet out.

How many sweets are there now?

I will count back from 50.

III

Numbers to 50

Discover

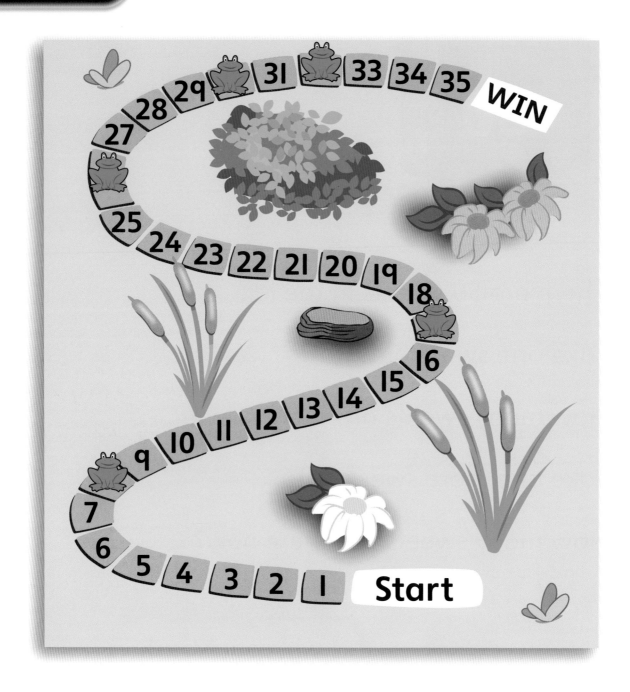

1 **a)** Count to 50 as a class.

b) What numbers are the frogs on?

Share

a)

I used this number grid to help me count to 50.

1	2	3	4	5	6	7	8	9	10
11	12	13	14	15	16	17	18	19	20
21	22	23	24	25	26	27	28	29	30
31	32	33	34	35	36	37	38	39	40
41	42	43	44	45	46	47	48	49	50

b)

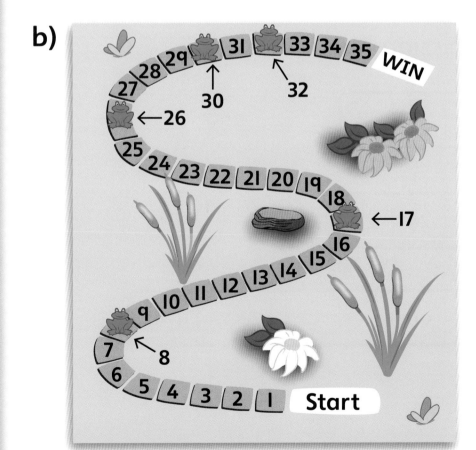

Think together

1 What are the missing numbers?

1	2	3	4	5	6	7	8	9	10
11	12	13	14	15		17	18	19	20
21		23	24	25	26	27	28	29	30
31	32	33	34	35	36	37	38	39	
41	42		44	45	46	47	48	49	50

2 What are the missing numbers?

a)

14	15	16		18

b)

21	22		24	25

c)

37		39	40		42	43	44	45

3 Ola is lost in the forest.

She must find her way from 34 to 45, in order.

Can you help her to find her way out?

CHALLENGE

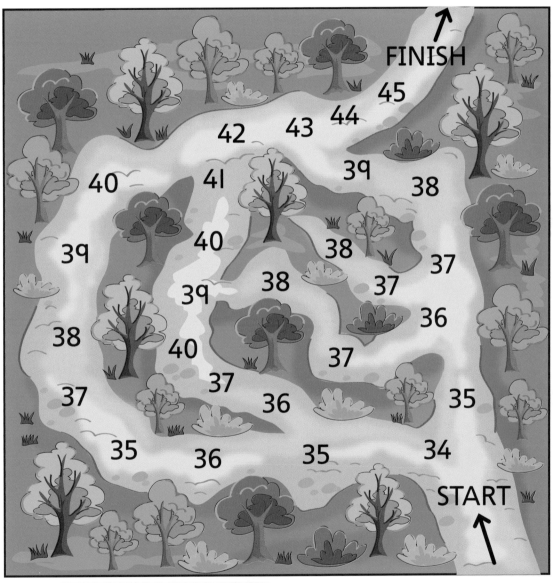

How did you help her find the way?

115

→ Practice book 1B p82

20, 30, 40 and 50

Discover

I have 30 counters.

I have 40 cubes.

30

Danny

Meg

1 **a)** Use 30 counters. Fill some ten frames.
How many can Danny fill?

b) Use 40 cubes. Make towers of 10. How many towers can Meg make?

Share

a)

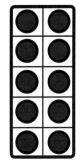 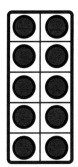

I know that 10 counters fit in a ten frame.

Danny can fill 3 ten frames with 30 counters.

b)

Meg can make 4 towers of 10 cubes.

Think together

1 Kat has put some straws into 10s.

How many straws does Kat have?

2 How many?

a)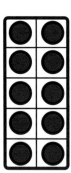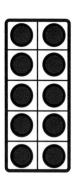

b)

3 Count in 10s to 50.

What do you notice about the numbers?

CHALLENGE

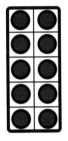 10

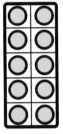 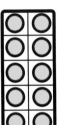 20

I notice something about the ten frames.

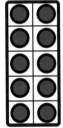 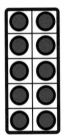 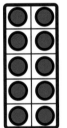 30

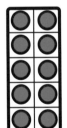 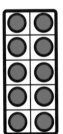 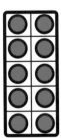 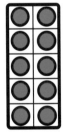 40

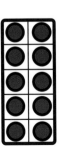 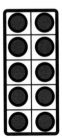 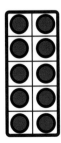 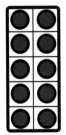 50

119

→ Practice book 1B p85

Count by making groups of 10s

Discover

1 **a)** A box holds 10 eggs.

How many egg boxes can you fill?

b) How many eggs are there in total?

Share

a)

I used counters for the eggs and ten frames for the boxes.

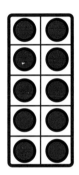 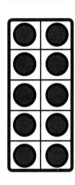 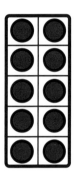

You can fill 3 egg boxes.

b)

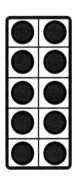 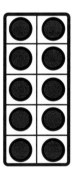

10   20   30   31 32 33 34 35

There are 35 eggs.

Think together

1 How many eggs are there in total?

2 How many apples?

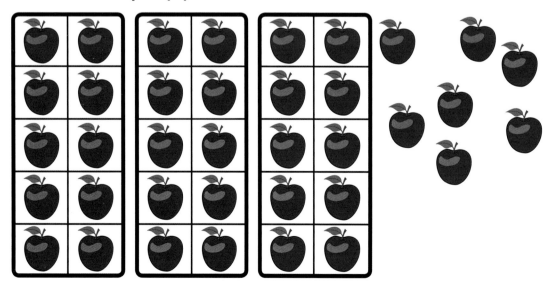

3 How many balls?

CHALLENGE

I will count the ones on the last ten frame.

I don't have to count them.

→ Practice book 1B p88

Groups of 10s and 1s

Discover

1

a) How many cakes?

b) Now how many cakes?

Share

a)

I didn't need to count the number in each box. I could see there were 10.

There are 25 cakes.

b)

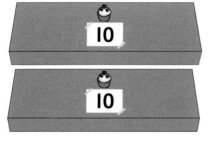

There are 25 cakes.

There are the same number. The boxes are closed but there are still 10 in each box.

125

Think together

1 How many eggs?

2 How many?

a)

b)

3 Tim is using a rekenrek.

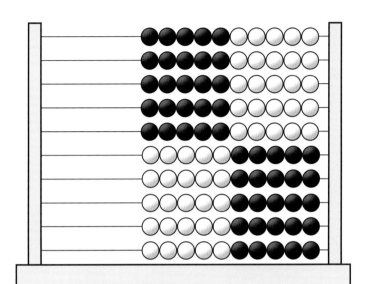

Tim makes this number.

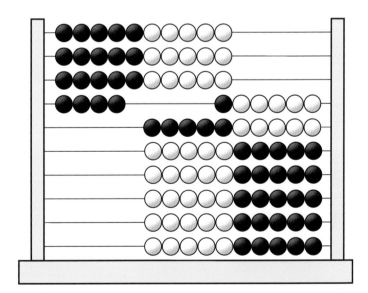

> I wonder if I could make some other numbers.

What number has he made?

127

Partition into 10s and 1s

Discover

1 **a)** Show that 34 is 3 tens and 4 ones.

b) Complete the part-whole model.

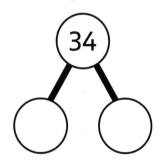

Share

a)

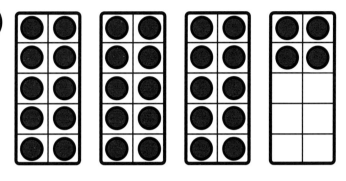

I showed it using some 10 frames.

I showed it on a bead string.

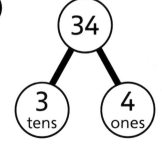

This shows that 34 is 3 tens and 4 ones.

b)

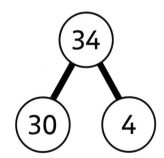

Think together

1 Write the numbers.

a)

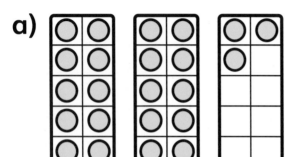

☐ tens and ☐ ones is ☐.

b)

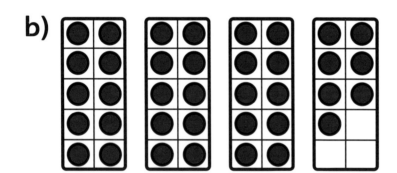

☐ tens and ☐ ones is ☐.

2 Complete the part-whole models.

a)

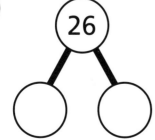

b)

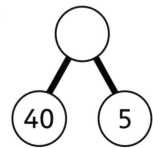

CHALLENGE

3 This shows 36 in different ways.

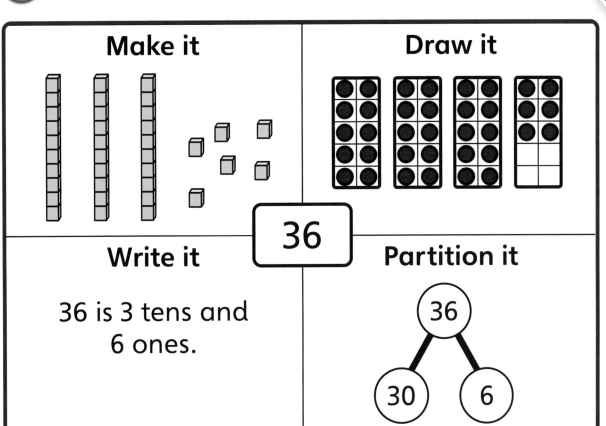

Make it

Draw it

36

Write it

36 is 3 tens and 6 ones.

Partition it

36

30   6

Draw grids like this to show 24 and 42.

I can make the number using different equipment.

I wonder if there are other ways I can write it too.

→ **Practice book 1B p94**

One more, one less

Discover

Amy

1 **a)** How many  on the wall?

b) Amy has one more.

How many now?

Share

a)

There are 10 in each row. I counted in 10s first.

There are 34 .

b)

One more than 34 is 35.

There are 35 .

I didn't have to count them one by one. I know one more than 34 is 35.

Think together

1

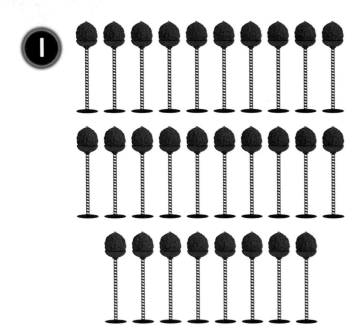

a) How many ?

b) One is knocked over.

How many now?

2 Here is 43.

a) What is one more than 43?

b) What is one less than 43?

3 Complete.

I more

37 ⬚

I more

49 ⬚

I less

⬚ 25

I can count to 50 so these numbers are easy to work out.

135

→ Practice book 1B p97

End of unit check

Your teacher will ask you these questions.

1 What is the missing number?

47	48	49	

A 410

B 48

C 50

D 15

2 How many eggs?

A 3

B 10

C 15

D 30

3 What number is shown?

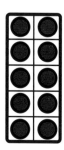  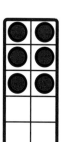

A 6

B 16

C 26

D 30

4 What is the missing number?

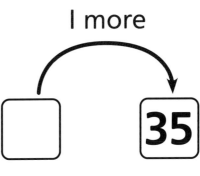

I more

35

A 34 **B** 35 **C** 36 **D** 25

Think!

Complete a grid like this and answer the questions.

Make it using addition	Draw it using objects
Complete 32	32 How many tens? ☐ How many ones? ☐

These words will help you.

ones   tens

part-whole

number track

137

→ Practice book 1B p100

Unit 9
Introducing length and height

In this unit we will ...
- ⚡ Compare lengths and heights of objects
- ⚡ Use non-standard units to measure objects
- ⚡ Measure with a ruler
- ⚡ Solve word problems about length

We can use cubes to help us compare the length of objects. Which is longer, the pen or the pencil?

We will need some maths words. Can you read them out loud?

long, longer, longest | measure | length

tall, taller, tallest | short, shorter, shortest

wide, wider, widest | thin, thinner, thinnest

compare | height

We use a ruler to measure lengths. How long is this pencil?

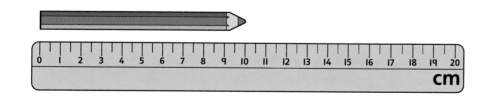

Compare lengths and heights

Discover

1 **a)** **Compare** the **heights** of Anya and Myra.

   Who is **shorter**, who is **taller**?

   b) Emily says she is **tallest**.

   Is she correct? How can they check?

Share

a)

Anya  Myra

I made sure that everyone was lined up next to each other.

Anya is shorter than Myra.

Myra is taller than Anya.

b)

Emily is on a ladder so she is higher. But she might not be taller. They need to line up next to each other to check.

Think together

1 Use these words to compare the skipping ropes.

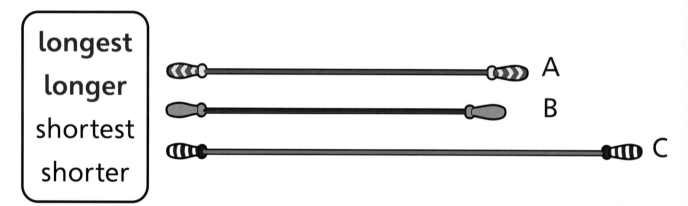

longest
longer
shortest
shorter

2 Complete drawings of flowers from shortest to tallest.

Shortest   Tallest

3 Find two leaves or twigs.

Which is longer, which is shorter?

longer

shorter

Which is **wider**, which is **thinner**?

wider

thinner

I will make sure I line them up carefully.

143

→ Practice book 1B p102

Measure length (non-standard units of measure)

Discover

1 **a)** Which is longer, the car or the fire engine?

b) How many cubes **long** is the car?

How many cubes long is the fire engine?

Share

a) The fire engine is longer than the car.

The car is shorter than the fire engine.

b)

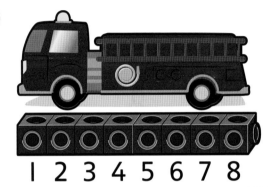

1 2 3 4 5 6 7 8

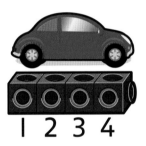

1 2 3 4

> I noticed that the fire engine is longer because there are more cubes.

The fire engine is 8 cubes long.

The car is 4 cubes long.

> I made sure that the cubes went from one end to the other.

145

Think together

1

The doll is ☐ cubes **tall**.

The teddy bear is ☐ cubes tall.

The teddy bear is _____ than the doll.

2

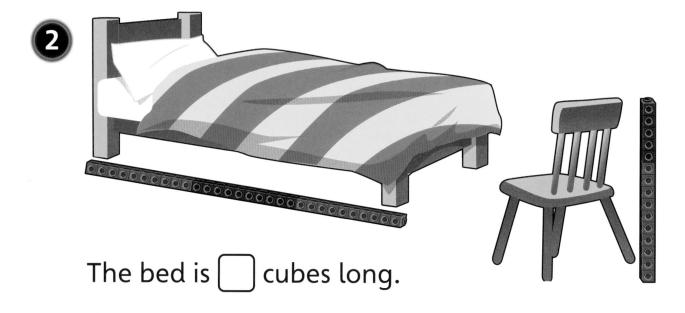

The bed is ☐ cubes long.

The chair is ☐ cubes tall.

3 Find objects in the classroom to complete the table.

Say how many cubes you used to measure each object.

	Fewer than 10 cubes	10 cubes	More than 10 cubes
Tall			
Long			

I will measure the object with cubes first then draw it.

147

Measure length (using a ruler)

Discover

1 a) Which is the longer piece of string?

Explain how both pieces of string can be
4 cubes long.

b) Use the ruler to **measure** both pieces of string.

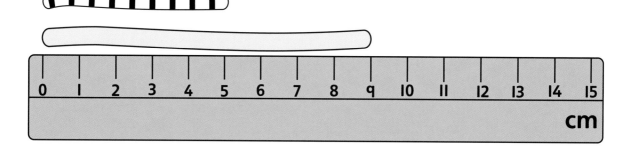

Share

a) is longer.

They are both 4 cubes long but the cubes are different sizes.

b)

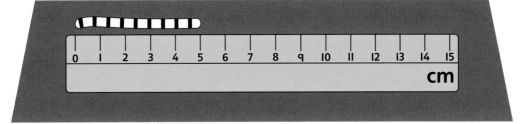

is 5 cm long.

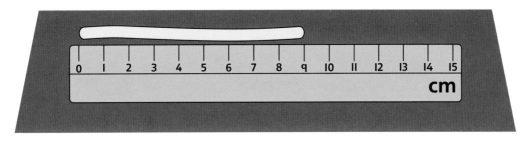

is 9 cm long.

A centimetre is about the same size as the width of your thumb: cm stands for centimetre.

cm

All cm are exactly the same **length**.

Think together

1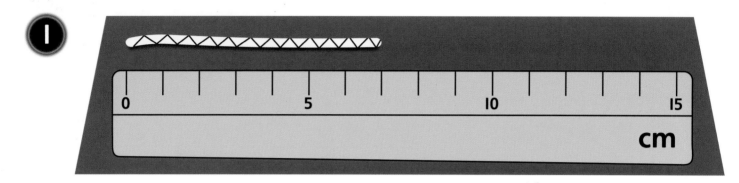

How long is the string?

The string is ☐ cm.

2 Measure the ribbons with a ruler.

a) The ribbon is ☐ cm.

b) The ribbon is ☐ cm.

c)

The ribbon is ☐ cm.

3 Find three objects you could draw in each box. Use a ruler to measure them.

CHALLENGE

Shorter than 10 cm	10 cm or longer	10 cm or taller

I found a rubber. It is 7 cm long. I will draw this in the first box.

My pencil case is 10 cm tall. I wonder if I can draw it in any box.

151

→ Practice book 1B p108

Solve word problems – length

Discover

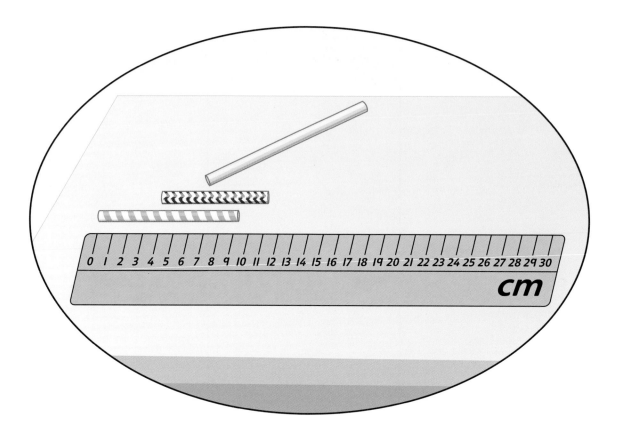

1 **a)** Work out the length of ▨▨▨▨▨▨▨▨▨▨ .

b) Order all the straws from shortest to longest.

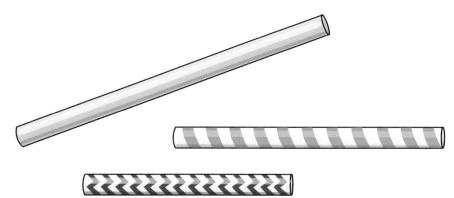

Share

a)

I moved the straw to start at zero.

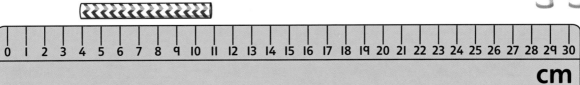

The length of 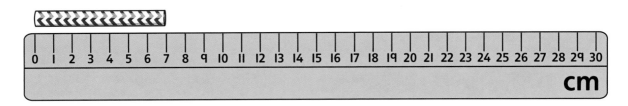 is 7 cm.

I lined up the ends and then compared the lengths.

b)

shortest
↓
longest

Think together

1 Kiko has two straws.

Kiko puts the straws together, end to end.

What is the total length?

2 Which toy train is 3 cm tall?

I wonder why they are not both 3 cm.

3 What is the difference in length between

the  and the ?

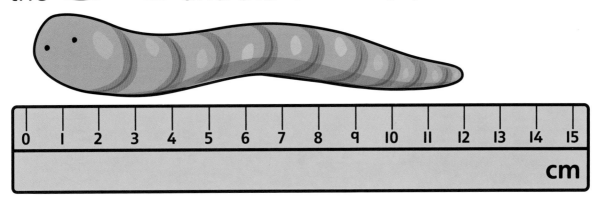

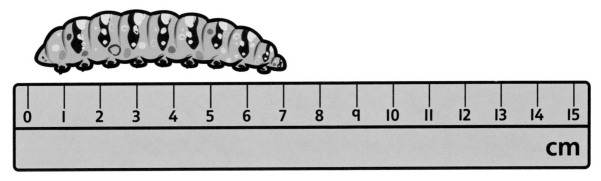

The difference in length is ☐ cm.

I think I need to do a subtraction for this question.

I am just going to count on.

155

End of unit check

Your teacher will ask you these questions.

1 Which statement is false?

A The 🐻 is taller than the 🐯.

B The 🐯 is the shortest.

C The 🦒 is shorter than the 🐻.

D The 🦒 is the tallest.

2 Which image shows the worm is 5 cubes long?

A
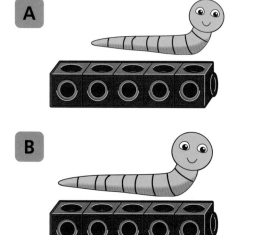

C
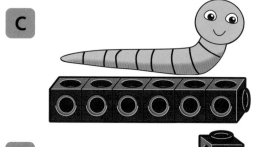

B

D
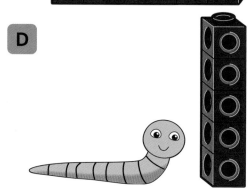

3 How tall is the mug?

Use a ruler.

A 4 cm   **B** 2 cm   **C** 3 cm   **D** 5 cm

4 How long is the straw?

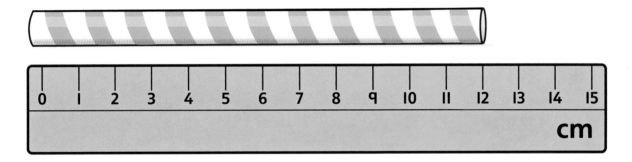

A 15 cm   **B** 12 cm   **C** 3 cm   **D** 18 cm

Think!

Which piece of string is longer? Explain your answer.

These words will help you.

| longer | shorter |
| curved | straight |

157

→ Practice book 1B p114

Unit 10
Introducing mass and capacity

In this unit we will ...
- ⚡ Compare the mass of objects
- ⚡ Weigh objects
- ⚡ Compare the capacity of objects
- ⚡ Measure capacity
- ⚡ Solve word problems about mass and capacity

This is a balance scale. We can use it to compare the mass of objects. Which item do you think is heavier?

We will need some maths words. Can you read them out loud?

heavier, heaviest   lighter, lightest

capacity   balance scales   full

empty   compare   weight, weigh   mass

balanced   measure   estimate

We can use glasses to measure capacity. Which jug had the most squash in it?

Heavier and lighter

Discover

Put the heavier one in the bag first.

James

1 a) James has a 🍍 and an apple.

Which is **heavier**?

b) Which is **lighter**, milk or  ?

160

Share

a)

I think the 🍍 feels heavier.

I used **balance scales** to compare the objects.

The 🍍 is down and the apple is up.

The 🍍 is heavier than the apple.

b)

The 🧴 is up and the milk is down.

The 🧴 is lighter than the milk.

Think together

1 Which is heavier? Which is lighter?

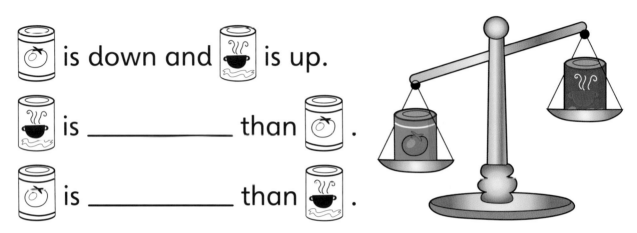

⊙ is down and ☕ is up.

☕ is _____ than ⊙ .

⊙ is _____ than ☕ .

2 Point to the heavier item on each scale.

What do you notice?

3 Who is correct?

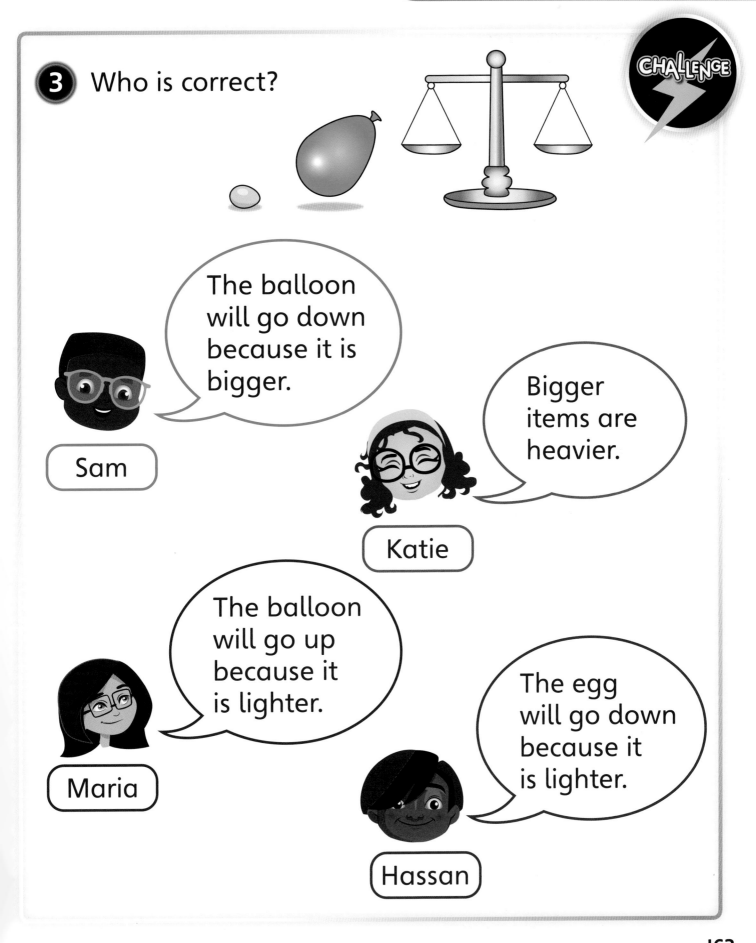

CHALLENGE

Sam: The balloon will go down because it is bigger.

Katie: Bigger items are heavier.

Maria: The balloon will go up because it is lighter.

Hassan: The egg will go down because it is lighter.

→ Practice book 1B p116

Measure mass

Discover

1 a) Hiro places one more cube on the scales.

Now the book balances the 10 cubes.

Is Hiro correct?
Is Joe correct?

b) Why does Lucy need fewer cubes than Hiro?

Share

a) There were 9 cubes.

Hiro adds one more cube.

The book balances 10 cubes.

Hiro is correct.

Joe should have used cubes of the same size to balance his book.

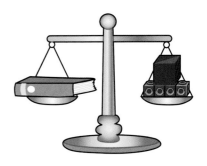

I know you must use all the same cubes to measure.

b) Lucy uses different cubes to **weigh** the book.

 are heavier than .

Lucy uses heavier cubes, so she does not need as many to balance the book.

Think together

1 Record the mass of the 👟.

has a mass of ☐ ▢.

has a mass of ☐ ◇.

has a mass of ☐ 🖍.

2 Copy and complete the table.

Object	Mass in 🎲
🔦	
	12
◼	
	1

3

CHALLENGE

How can you balance the scales?

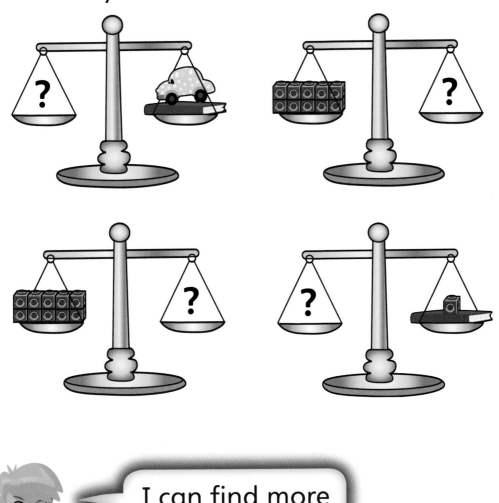

I can find more than one way.

→ **Practice book 1B p119**

Compare mass

Discover

1 **a)** Which box goes on the top shelf?

Which box goes on the bottom shelf?

b) Put the boxes in order from **heaviest** to **lightest**.

Share

a)

I put the masses in order by comparing the number of cubes.

The mass of the is 10 cubes.

The mass of the is 13 cubes.

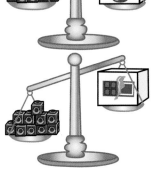
The mass of the is less than 10 cubes.
We know it is lighter because it is up on the scales.

The drinks go on the bottom shelf
The chocolate goes on the top shelf.

b) Heaviest   Lightest

Think together

1

Complete the sentences.

a) ⬡ is heavier than _____ .

b) ⬡ is _____ than ⬡ .

c) ⬡ is equal to _____ .

2

Work out the correct shelf for each box.

Heaviest items on bottom. Lightest items on top.

3 What is the mass of each of the toys?

Can you see more than one possible answer?

→ Practice book 1B p122

Full and empty

Discover

1 **a)** Which glass is **full**?

Which glass is **empty**?

b) Which of these does Molly want?

172

Share

a)

This glass is full.

This glass is empty.

b) Molly wants less than .

I compared the glasses by looking for the level of squash.

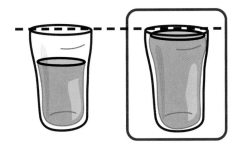

This glass has more than .

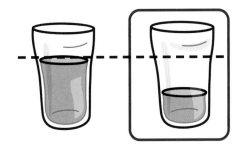

This glass has less than .

Molly wants this glass.

Think together

1 Put these in order, from empty to full.

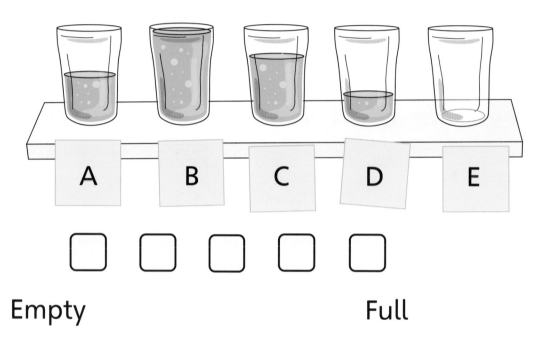

A   B   C   D   E

☐ ☐ ☐ ☐ ☐

Empty   Full

2 Molly pours ⬚ into a ⬚ .

Fred pours ⬚ into a ⬚ .

Does ⬚ or ⬚ hold more?

③ CHALLENGE

I would like an ice cube, please.

I would like a full glass of juice, please.

I would like more than a half full glass of juice, please.

Fred

Molly

Sam

Which drinks could each person have?

I think there is more than one answer.

I wonder if there are any drinks that no one wants.

175

→ Practice book 1B p125

Measure capacity

Discover

I used 20 spoons to fill the bucket.

Mr Chabra

Fred

Ava

1 a) **Estimate** how many cups of sand will fill the bucket.

b) Estimate how many spades Ava will use to fill the bucket.

Share

a)

Capacity means how much a container can hold.

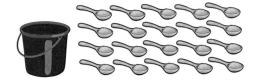 20 spoons fill the bucket.

The bucket has a capacity of 20 spoons.

Fred will need fewer cups to fill the bucket.

About 10 cups of sand fill the bucket.

b) The spade holds a lot of sand.

Ava will need fewer than 10.

3 is a good estimate.

 3 spades fill the bucket.

Think together

1 Fred and Ava help each other to fill the bucket.

I put in 4 spoons.

Fred

I put in 5 spoons.

Ava

How many spoons fill the bucket?

2

Copy and complete the table.

Container	How many needed to fill
	15

3 Who is right?

CHALLENGE

This jug holds 6 glasses.

Mr Chabra

This jug holds 8 glasses.

Mrs Hodge

This jug holds 5 glasses.

Mrs Shaw

179

Compare capacity

Discover

1 **a)** Complete the sentences.

| A | B | C |

☐ is filled by 2 cups.

☐ is filled by 15 cups.

☐ is filled by 5 cups.

b) Put the containers in order of capacity, from greatest to smallest.

Share

a)

I know that 15 > 5 > 2, so the largest container is filled by 15 cups.

 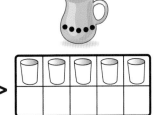 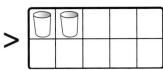

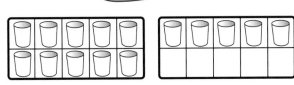

15 > 5 > 2

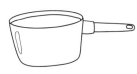 is filled by 15 cups.

 is filled by 5 cups.

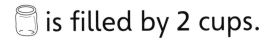 is filled by 2 cups.

b)

Greatest capacity 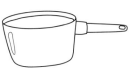   Smallest capacity

181

Think together

1 Match the buckets to the cups.

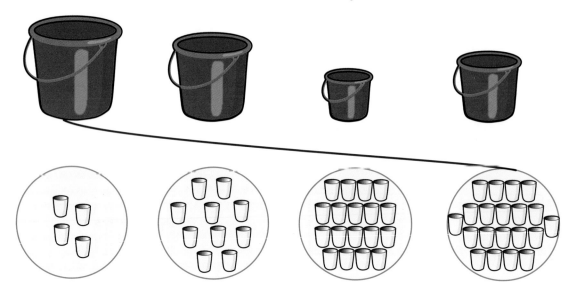

2 Put the containers in order.

Start with the container with the greatest capacity.

Container	Fills
	🥤🥤🥤
	🥤🥤🥤🥤🥤 🥤🥤
	🥤🥤🥤🥤🥤

3 Some glasses are filled from jugs.

Order the jugs from smallest to greatest capacity.

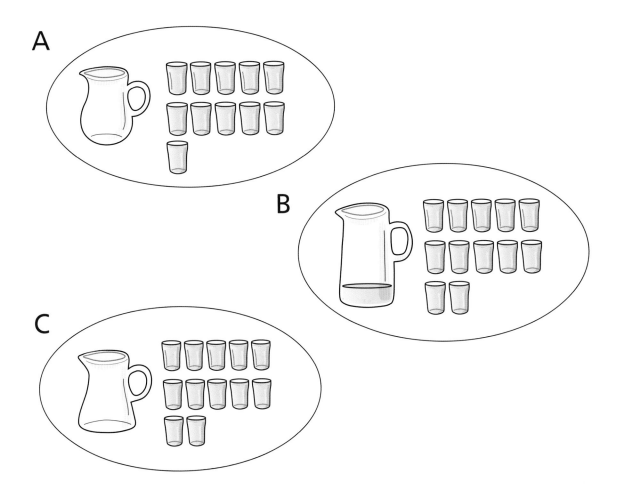

A

B

C

There is still some water in jug B, but the glasses are all full.

183

Solve word problems – mass and capacity

Discover

The jug holds 10 ▯.

The pan holds 6 ▯.

1 a) The pan is filled with milk from the jug.

How many ▯ are there left in the jug?

b) A full jug and a full pan are poured into a ◡.

How many ▯ will there be in the ◡ ?

Share

I know that there were 10  in the full jug. Then some was poured out.

a)

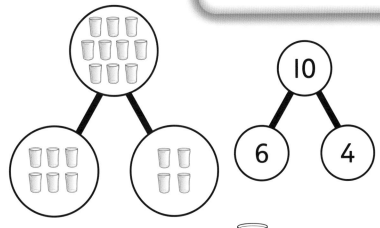

10

6   4

This is a subtraction. I broke the whole into two parts.

There were 10  in the jug.

6 glasses fill the  .

10 – 6 = 4.

There are 4  left in the jug.

b)

    10 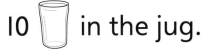 in the jug.

 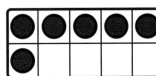   6 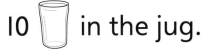 in the pan.

10 + 6 = 16

16 will be in the  .

Think together

1 How many cups of rice will be in the pan?

 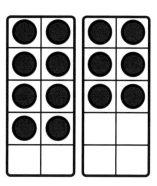

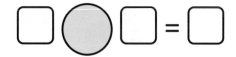

There are ☐ cups of rice in the pan.

2 How much does the smaller box weigh?

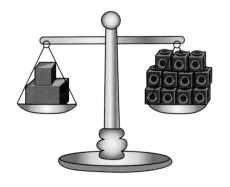 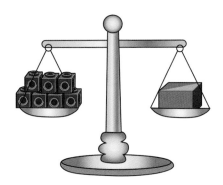 

☐ ◯ ☐ = ☐

The smaller box weighs the same as ☐ cubes.

186

CHALLENGE

3 **a)**

How many sheep balance 1 horse?

I will use 1 cube to represent the **weight** of 1 sheep. Then I will work out how many cubes represent 1 goat.

b)

How many cats balance 1 goose?

→ **Practice book 1B p134**

End of unit check

Your teacher will ask you these questions.

1 Which is true?

A  is heavier than △.

B  weighs the same as △.

C △ is lighter than □.

D △ is heavier than □.

2 Which weighs 8 □ ?

A   B   C   D

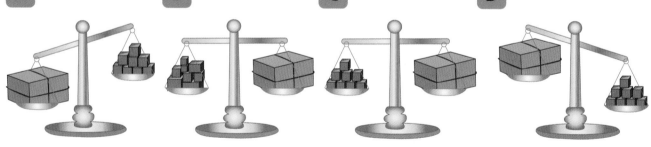

3 Which jug has more than ?

A    B    C    D

4 How many cubes balance one 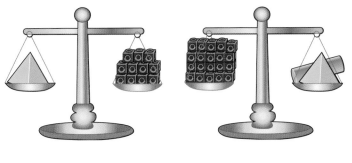?

A 20   **B** 11   **C** 1   **D** 9

Think!

How many blocks will 10 glasses of water weigh?

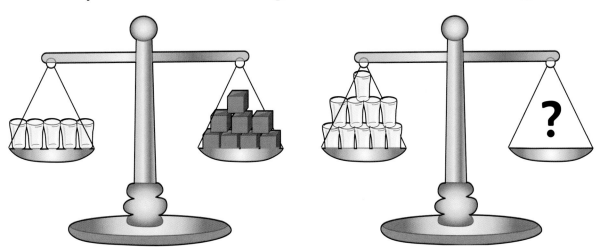

Explain how you know.

These words will help you.

lighter   heavier

fewer   more

189

→ **Practice book 1B p137**

I like it when we find different ways to solve the same problem.

Me too! We can all learn from each other.

What do we know now?

Can you do all these things?

⚡ Work with numbers up to 20

⚡ Add and subtract numbers within 20

⚡ Work with numbers up to 50

⚡ Measure and compare length and height

⚡ Measure and compare mass and capacity

It's ok to get things wrong. It helps us learn.

Now you're ready for the next books!

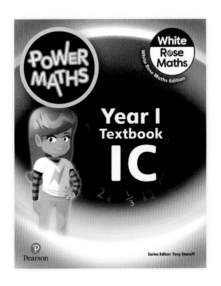

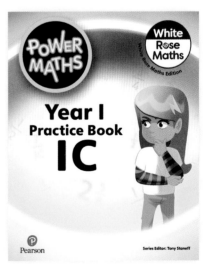

Published by Pearson Education Limited, 80 Strand, London, WC2R 0RL.

www.pearsonschools.co.uk

Text © Pearson Education Limited 2017, 2022
Edited by Pearson and Florence Production Ltd
First edition edited by Pearson, Little Grey Cells Publishing Services and Haremi Ltd
Designed and typeset by Pearson, Florence Production Ltd and PDQ Digital Media Solutions Ltd
First edition designed and typeset by Kamae Design
Original illustrations © Pearson Education Limited 2017, 2022
Illustrated by Nadene Naude, Adam Linley, Laura Arias, Jim Peacock, Nigel Dobbyn and Phil Corbett at Beehive
Illustration, Emily Skinner at Graham-Cameron Illustration, Kamae Design, Florence Production Ltd, and
PDQ Digital Media Solutions Ltd
Cover design by Pearson Education Ltd
Front and back cover illustrations by Will Overton at Advocate Art and Nadene Naude at Beehive Illustration

Series Editor: Tony Staneff
Lead author: Josh Lury
Consultants (first edition): Professor Jian Liu and Professor Zhang Dan

The rights of Tony Staneff and Josh Lury to be identified as authors of this work have been asserted by them in
accordance with the Copyright, Designs and Patents Act 1988.

First published 2017
This edition first published 2022

26 25 24 23 22
10 9 8 7 6 5 4 3 2 1

British Library Cataloguing in Publication Data
A catalogue record for this book is available from the British Library

ISBN 978 1 292 41968 8

Printed in the UK by Bell & Bain Ltd, Glasgow

For Power Maths resources go to
www.activelearnprimary.co.uk

Note from the publisher
Pearson has robust editorial processes, including answer and fact checks, to ensure the accuracy of the content in this
publication, and every effort is made to ensure this publication is free of errors. We are, however, only human, and
occasionally errors do occur. Pearson is not liable for any misunderstandings that arise as a result of errors in this
publication, but it is our priority to ensure that the content is accurate. If you spot an error, please do contact us at
resourcescorrections@pearson.com so we can make sure it is corrected.